MIRIAM SCHLEIN
DISCOVERING
DINOSAUR BABIES
ILLUSTRATED BY MARGARET COLBERT

FOUR WINDS PRESS   NEW YORK

Collier Macmillan Canada   Toronto

Maxwell Macmillan International Publishing Group

New York   Oxford   Singapore   Sydney

The CRETACEOUS PERIOD gets its name from the Latin word *creta*, meaning "chalk." There were chalky layers on some seabeds during that time.

The JURASSIC PERIOD gets its name from the kind of rocks formed during that time in the Jura Mountains in France and Switzerland.

The TRIASSIC PERIOD gets its name from the Latin word *trias*, meaning "three," because there were three rock layers formed in Germany at that time.

THE MESOZOIC ERA

CRETACEOUS PERIOD

65 million years ago

Pinacosaurus

Protoceratops

Hypselosaurus

Psittacosaurus

JURASSIC PERIOD

136 million years ago (approximate date)

Apatosaurus

Allosaurus

193 million years ago

TRIASSIC PERIOD

Mussaurus
(projected size of adult)

225 million years ago

Dinosaurs lived in the time of the earth's past called the Mesozoic (mez-uh-ZOE-ick) era. It is divided into three periods: Triassic (try-ASS-ick), the earliest; Jurassic (jur-ASS-ick), the middle; and Cretaceous (kruh-TAY-shuss), the latest. This time line shows in which period each of the different dinosaurs in this book lived.

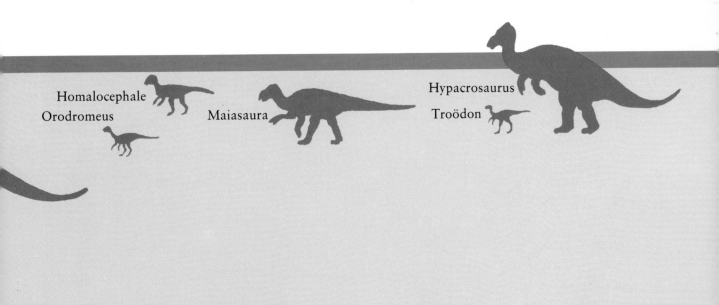

Homalocephale
Orodromeus
Maiasaura
Hypacrosaurus
Troödon

WHERE THESE DINOSAURS HAVE BEEN FOUND

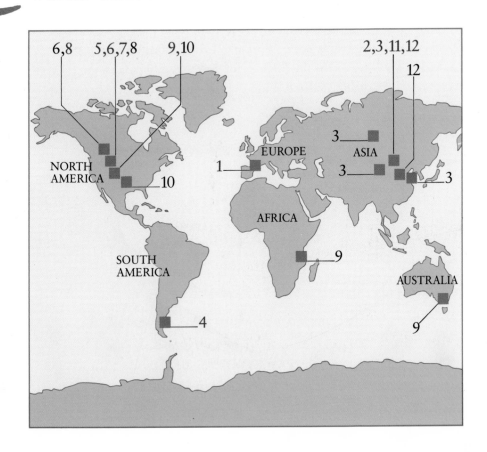

1. Hypselosaurus
2. Protoceratops
3. Psittacosaurus
4. Mussaurus
5. Maiasaura
6. Troödon
7. Orodromeus
8. Hypacrosaurus
9. Allosaurus
10. Apatosaurus
11. Homalocephale
12. Pinacosaurus

Numerals in red indicate
the particular finds
discussed in this book.

To my good friend Ned,
who helps me keep these
animals plausible
—M.C.

Special thanks to David D. Gillette, Ph.D., of the Southwest
Paleontology Foundation, Inc., for checking the facts in this book.

Grateful acknowledgment is made to John R. Horner and James
Gorman for permission to adapt an illustration from their book
Digging Dinosaurs (New York: Workman, 1988) in art on page
15, and to the Museum of the Rockies for permission to adapt
their picture of a reconstructed embryo in art on page 26.

Four Winds Press, Macmillan Publishing Company
866 Third Avenue, New York, NY 10022
Collier Macmillan Canada, Inc.
1200 Eglinton Avenue East, Suite 200, Don Mills, Ontario M3C 3N1

Printed and bound in Hong Kong   First American Edition   10 9 8 7 6 5 4 3 2 1

The text of this book is set in 13 point Sabon.
The illustrations are rendered in gouache.
LIBRARY OF CONGRESS CATALOGING-IN-PUBLICATION DATA
Schlein, Miriam. Discovering dinosaur babies/Miriam Schlein; illustrated by
Margaret Colbert. — 1st American ed.   p.   cm.
Summary: Explains what paleontologists have been able to determine about how
the different varieties of dinosaurs cared for their young.
ISBN 0-02-778091-0
1. Dinosaurs – Infancy – Juvenile literature. [1. Dinosaurs. 2. Animals – Infancy.
3. Fossils.] I. Colbert, Margaret, ill. II. Title.
QE862.D5S35 1991 567.9'1 – dc 20   89-23496 CIP AC

Did dinosaur mothers and fathers take care of their babies? Did they feed them? Protect them? Help them grow up? Did baby dinosaurs *need* help in growing up?

To answer these questions, paleontologists (people who study prehistoric life) have to be like detectives. They have to get their information from clues—only their clues are millions of years old. The clues are in the form of fossil remains, such as dinosaur bones, teeth, skulls, and footprints, that have turned to stone.

Using these clues, we've learned a lot about dinosaurs. The problem was, until recently, there were hardly any clues about baby dinosaurs.

Why? First of all, baby bones, being small, are less likely to be found than big dinosaur bones. Also, because baby bones are not so thick and sturdy, they tend to break up into tiny bits. This makes it even harder to find them. Often they just look like little pebbles.

But recently there has been a burst of new discoveries, giving us more information about baby dinosaurs than we ever knew before. What are the new clues? How were they discovered? What do they tell us? Let's trace the clues, one by one.

HYPSELOSAURUS

Back in the 1860s, dinosaur eggs were found in France and Spain. They were jumbo eggs—twelve inches long and ten inches wide. The big, bumpy eggs look more like lopsided soccer balls than eggs. Scientists think they are the eggs of the forty-foot-long sauropod *Hypselosaurus* (hip-sel-oh-SOAR-us), which lived 80 million years ago. They are the biggest dinosaur eggs ever found. They were just lying on the ground in rows. *Hypselosaurus* mothers may have taken care of their babies—but if they did, they left no sign of it.

The first real clue came in 1923. An expedition led by Roy Chapman Andrews of the American Museum of Natural History found dinosaur eggs in Mongolia. These eight-inch-long eggs were in sand nests. They were laid by *Protoceratops* (pro-toe-SAIR-uh-tops), a small (six-foot-long) dinosaur that lived 80 million years ago.

We knew that baby dinosaurs—at least some of them—were hatched from eggs. This was not a big surprise. Dinosaurs were reptiles. And most reptiles (though not all) *do* lay eggs.

A turtle mother lays eggs, covers them up, and goes off. The babies never see their mother.

An alligator mother does more. She lays eggs in a nest, but she doesn't go away. She stays nearby to guard it. She will attack anything that comes close enough to threaten the nest's safety.

When the alligator mother hears peeping, she uncovers the nest. And she stays around for a week or so, to see that no harm comes as the babies go down to the water for the first time. Then the babies are on their own.

Reptiles are animals that have a backbone, breathe air, and have a scaly body covering instead of hair or feathers. Among today's reptiles are crocodiles, alligators, turtles, snakes, and lizards.

Alligator mother and her young

What did the *Protoceratops* mother do? Did she lay her eggs, then leave them, like a turtle? We don't think so. Here is the clue. Close to the nests were skeletons of more than one hundred *Protoceratops*. There were

adults and young of all ages, including newly hatched babies. This is a strong clue that *Protoceratops* did stay nearby to guard her eggs and her babies.

PSITTACOSAURUS

A few years later another expedition from the American Museum of Natural History found the remains of two baby dinosaurs in Mongolia. These belonged to a kind of dinosaur called *Psittacosaurus* (sit-ak-oh-SOAR-us), which means "parrot lizard." It was given this name because it had a sharp, down-turned jaw that looked like the beak of a parrot.

Psittacosaurus was a small dinosaur (two and a half to five feet long) that lived 110 million years ago. The babies' skulls were tiny, about one inch long. The entire baby was probably around nine inches long— about the size of a hamster.

The *Psittacosaurus* babies were not newly hatched. We know this because the teeth in the tiny skulls were already worn down. It shows they had been eating tough vegetation. The leg bones were well formed. These are two clues that the babies may have been active self-feeders right after they were hatched.

MUSSAURUS PATAGONICUS

In 1977, in a part of Argentina called Patagonia, paleontologist José Bonaparte found six baby dinosaur skeletons plus two small eggs, all in a nest.

Family: Mussauridae
Genus: *Mussaurus*
Species: *patagonicus*

These were the smallest dinosaurs ever found. For this reason, Bonaparte named the species *Mussaurus patagonicus* (moos-SOAR-us pat-uh-GOAN-i-kus), which means "mouse lizard of Patagonia."

Their skulls were about the size of a quarter. The body of the largest one measured only eight inches.

It was an important discovery because it showed that after they were hatched, these babies stayed together in the nest. Does it mean that their mother was going to come back and feed them? We don't know. Maybe soon more clues will be found.

Mussaurus lived about 200 million years ago. No adult has been found yet, but scientists think an adult *Mussaurus* may have been about ten feet long.

Then, in 1978, John Horner and Robert Makela began to make breakthrough discoveries that told us more about dinosaur babies than we had ever known before.

The two friends had been fossil hunting in Montana. They did this every summer, on vacation. (Horner had grown up in Montana. He found his first dinosaur fossil when he was seven.)

It all began when a woman named Marion Brandvold showed them some tiny bones she had found. Horner picked one up. It was only an inch long, and it was broken. Still, Horner had a hunch he was holding part of the leg bone of a baby hadrosaur (HAD-ro-soar). Hadrosaurs were the kind of dinosaur we sometimes call "duckbills" because of their flat, ducklike snout.

Brandvold took Horner and Makela to the ranch near Choteau, Montana, where she had found the bones. Digging in the dry land, they soon found a big mud nest. In it was a jumble of bones. Sorting them out, the fossil hunters saw they had the remains of fifteen three-foot-long baby hadrosaurs.

The nest was about seven feet wide. It was built up from the ground. Its center was scooped out like a three-foot-deep bowl. Probably the nest had been made by the mother hadrosaur, who dug it out by shaping it with her front feet and perhaps her mouth.

When discovered, the nest was underground. How do we know it was really a nest? Here is the clue. The inside of the "bowl" was of green mudstone (mud hardened into stone). All around it was red mudstone. According to Horner, this is what probably happened. After the babies died (*why* they died, nobody knows), mud and silt drifted down from a stream, filling the nest with what later turned into hardened green mudstone. The nest outline was clear.

The babies were not newly hatched. Some of their teeth were worn down by more than half. This shows they had been eating for a while. And it looked as if they had spent a lot of time—maybe all their time— right in the nest, because the eggshells they hatched from were trampled to small bits.

How did the babies get their food? Did they go out for it themselves? Or were they taken out by their mother to forage for food? Horner doesn't think either is likely. Little ones going out on their own would have been snapped up in a minute by some hungry predator. Even going out with their mother would have been risky. Could she guard fifteen babies and herd them all back?

But there is a third possibility. John Horner thinks the babies probably stayed in the nest, and their mother or both parents brought food back to them, the way bird parents do. They could have carried leaves and berries stuffed in their big "cheek pouches."

This would mean much more parenting than anyone ever thought dinosaurs did. So right now, not all experts agree with Horner on this. Maybe someday more clues will give us a definite answer.

We know what hadrosaurs ate because a mummified hadrosaur was found, and there were twigs, seeds, fruit, and pine needles in her stomach.

Nest "bowl" with baby hadrosaur bones

Not far from the nest, Laurie Trexler (Marion Brandvold's stepdaughter) found the skull of an adult hadrosaur. Horner and Makela examined it. They saw it was different from the skulls of other kinds of hadrosaurs. This meant the babies were of a never-before-discovered species of hadrosaur.

Horner and Makela named it *Maiasaura peeblesorum* (my-uh-SOAR-uh pee-bull-SOAR-um). *Maiasaura* means "good mother lizard." *Peeblesorum* is for James and John Peebles, who owned the ranch where the fossils were found. *Maiasaura* lived about 80 million years ago.

Family:
Hadrosauridae
Genus: *Maiasaura*
Species: *peeblesorum*

For the next six summers, Horner and Makela came back to the site. Now they had student volunteers to help them. They camped there all summer in tents and tepees. It was slow going... searching, digging, then freeing the delicate bones using ice picks or needles. Each year they made more discoveries and learned more about baby *Maiasaura*.

The skull of *Maiasaura*
compared to that of another hadrosaur,
Kritosaurus (red outline)

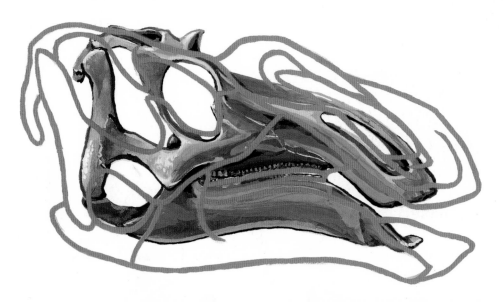

Volunteer Amy Luthin found one nest with smaller babies in it, only fourteen inches long. Their teeth were not worn down at all. This shows they had been recently hatched. Other nests had unhatched eggs in them. The eggs were eight inches long. They were always laid in a circle, tips tilting inward, with the big end up. Maybe it was easier for the babies to peck their way out that way.

The nests were found in groups. This is a clue that *Maiasaura*, like penguins, nested together in colonies. Horner and Makela noticed something else interesting. The nests were all the same distance apart — about twenty-three feet. Why?

Eggs have to be incubated (kept warm). Birds sit on their eggs to do this. But how could a twenty-five-foot-long mother *Maiasaura* sit on her eggs? She weighed two tons. She would break them. So, they figured, *Maiasaura* sat *beside* her nest. Twenty-three feet would give her just enough space to do this. To keep the eggs warm, she probably covered them with vegetation.

Sitting there, she could be on the lookout for danger: lizards or small mammals who would steal an egg when they could.

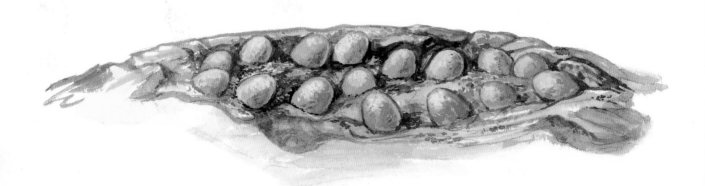

Groups of nests were found on different levels or "time horizons." (Fossils from a deeper level are generally from an earlier time.) This shows that the area was probably a traditional nesting ground—a place that the dinosaurs came back to, year after year, to lay their eggs, the way penguins do today.

The smallest nestlings (babies in nests) were fourteen inches long. The largest were about forty inches. How long did it take them to grow to that size?

Dinosaurs were reptiles. Reptiles of today are cold-blooded. Cold-blooded animals usually grow slowly. It takes a baby alligator a year to double its size.

"Cold-blooded" animals have a low body temperature that goes up or down according to the temperature of their surroundings.

Does this mean *Maiasaura* babies stayed in their nests more than a year? No animal we know of stays in the nest that long. Horner thinks it means something else — that *Maiasaura* babies grew very fast.

Warm-blooded creatures grow fast. It takes a baby bird only a month or two to double in size. The large size of some of the *Maiasaura* nestlings is a clue that *Maiasaura* might have been warm-blooded like mammals and birds, rather than cold-blooded like reptiles.

"Warm-blooded" animals (birds and mammals) have a high body temperature that stays pretty steady regardless of their surroundings.

For many years, scientists thought all dinosaurs were cold-blooded. Now there are scientists who say that perhaps some dinosaurs, unlike other reptiles, may have been warm-blooded. *Maiasaura* has given another clue that this might be true.

Maiasaura had no weapons like horns or protective armorlike bony plates. So they counted on safety in numbers, and traveled in herds. They might have warned one another of danger by making loud, buglelike sounds. Hadrosaurs had a hollow area in the skull that may have helped to produce sound by acting as a resonating chamber.

Judging by the remains that were found, herds seem to have been made up of adults plus young ones ten feet long or smaller. Where were the in-between-sized maiasaurs?

It's possible that the young needed the protection of adults only until they reached a certain size. Then, they might have split off and formed herds of their own. (Adolescent male elephants do this today.)

Near the nesting area, the fossil-hunting crew uncovered, bit by bit, the remains of a tremendous herd. The bones covered an area of more than one mile by one-quarter mile. It was the remains of about ten thousand *Maiasaura*.

What killed so many dinosaurs all at once? They were probably killed by the gases, smoke, and flame of a giant volcanic eruption. A clue to this is the layer of volcanic ash that covered the bones.

TROÖDON

On July 12, 1979, Horner, Makela, and thirteen student volunteers had just started a new summer of fossil hunting on the Peebles ranch. Two unusual things happened that day. First, some surveyors came along and started sticking little flags into the ground. They were about to do some blasting for an oil company. Second, student volunteer Fran Tannenbaum found a new kind of dinosaur egg lying on top of a small hill. It was not a *Maiasaura* egg. It was four inches long and bumpy. Soon the fossil hunters found more eggs. They named the spot Egg Mountain.

Luckily, John Horner was able to convince the oil surveyors to detour around this spot. Then he and his crew began to search Egg Mountain. The eggs they found were not in nests. They were lined up on their sides, in two rows. They were not covered by vegetation, but seem to have been warmed by the heat of the sun. In one, there was an embryo (an unhatched baby). But it was too small to identify. Nearby, they found a *Troödon* (TROE-o-don) tooth. So Horner thinks these might be the eggs of *Troödon*, a small, swift, flesh-eating dinosaur that lived around the same time as *Maiasaura*.

Troödon tooth

ORODROMEUS MAKELAI

Egg Mountain was made up of hard limestone. The crew could not break through with pick and shovel. So they used a jackhammer. Digging straight down, they soon found eggs and baby skeletons of a type of hypsilophodont (hip-sih-LO-fo-dont).

Herd of hypsilophodonts

Hypsilophodonts were small (eight-foot-long), fast-moving dinosaurs. They were among the speed runners of the dinosaur world. Holding their long tails straight out for balance, they ran along on their toes.

The hypsilophodont eggs found on Egg Mountain were about six inches long. They were laid in a spiral, wide end up. Most clutches (groups of eggs) were an even dozen. But some had twenty-four eggs. Those might have been nests shared by two mothers. The clutches were in groups, showing that hypsilopho-donts, like *Maiasaura*, nested in colonies. And they were found on different "time horizons," showing that the area was a traditional nesting ground—one that these dinosaurs returned to year after year.

Troödon(?)   Egg Mountain hypsilophodont   *Maiasaura*

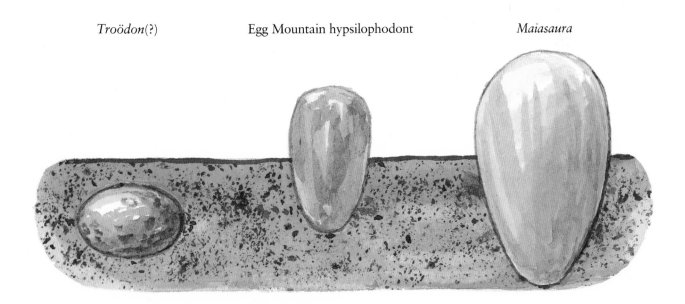

Remains of different-sized babies were found. The interesting thing is, not even the smallest ones were found inside a nest. And the egg bottoms in the nests were all intact. These are two signs that maybe the babies left the nest right away, and never went back in. If they had, the eggshells would have been mashed into small bits, like the *Maiasaura* eggshells. This is a clue that the hypsilophodont babies were the kind of baby we call *precocial*.

This makes sense. Unlike *Maiasaura*, hypsilophodonts were fast and could run from danger. Hypsilophodonts were also smaller, so hiding was easier for them. No adult hypsilophodont remains were found near the babies. (But teeth of *Albertosaurus* were found—a twenty-six-foot *Tyrannosaurus*-like carnivore.)

Horner's crew also found eggs with embryos inside. These were studied with a CAT-scan X-ray. The embryo thighs were long. The legs looked strong. This was a clue that the hypsilophodont babies may have been fast runners right from the start.

Horner examined the bones carefully. He saw something else. The bones had lots of blood vessels. That is a sign of a fast-growing animal. So hypsilophodonts, like *Maiasaura*, might have been warm-blooded. No one is sure of this.

Precocial (pri-KOE-shul) means babies that become independent soon after they are hatched or born. Babies who are helpless when young—like pandas or humans—are called *altricial* (al-TRISH-ul).

Reconstruction of an Egg Mountain hypsilophodont embryo

He also compared the hypsilophodont embryos with *Maiasaura* embryos. The *Maiasaura* embryo bones were not as well developed—another clue that *Maiasaura* babies were more helpless, and probably needed more care from their parents.

Horner named this species of hypsilophodont *Orodromeus makelai* (or-oh-DROE-me-us MAK-a-lie). *Orodromeus*, the genus name, means "mountain runner." The species name, *makelai*, is to honor his friend Bob Makela, who shared in so many of the discoveries.

Family:
Hypsilophodontidae
Genus: *Orodromeus*
Species: *makelai*

Adult *Albertosaurus*
and young
Orodromeus makelai

Near Egg Mountain, the crew found another nesting ground. They named this one "Egg Island." It is dry and dusty nowadays in this part of Montana, but it was not that way 80 million years ago. Both nesting sites were on small islands, surrounded by a shallow salt lake. (We know this because of ripple marks left by the water, and remains of snails and clams.) The lake existed only in the rainy season, creating these small islands. There were fewer predators on an island. It was a safer place for young dinosaurs to grow up.

The land looked different in other ways, too. A big inland sea called the Western Interior Cretaceous Seaway divided North America into two parts. Down by the sea were swamps and marshlands. Farther west, toward the Rocky Mountains, were drier

highlands. That's where *Maiasaura* and *Orodromeus* nested. Paleontologists called this area the Two Medicine Formation.

Remains of young ceratopsians (horned dinosaurs) have also been found here. In fact, four out of five fossils found in this highland area were those of young dinosaurs. It's a strong clue that this location might have been the nesting ground for a number of different dinosaurs.

This gives us another possible answer to the question of why, until now, so few baby dinosaur fossils were found. The fossil hunters were expecting to find them where they found most large dinosaur bones—in places that were once low, marshy areas. We see now that young dinosaurs—at least some of them—may have grown up on higher grounds.

In 1986, at a place called Devil's Gulch in Alberta, Canada, more baby dinosaur remains were found. It started when a high school student named Wendy Sloboda found some dinosaur egg bits near her home. She called the experts at the University of Calgary. A field crew came to search the area. Soon a baby toe bone was found. Then Wendy spotted a footprint showing the skin from the bottom of a hadrosaur foot.

Later on, paleontologist Philip Currie found hadrosaur nests and eggs—the first dinosaur nests ever found in Canada. Some broken eggs showed fully developed embryos eighteen inches long. Currie picked one up. Every part of the skeleton was still in place. He could see the teeth and the small spine. It was the most perfectly preserved dinosaur embryo ever found. It dates from 73 million years ago.

Again, the nests were in groups, on different time horizons—more evidence that some dinosaurs nested in colonies in traditional nesting grounds.

The Devil's Gulch hadrosaur was named *Hypacrosaurus* (hip-ak-roe-SOAR-us). It was different from *Maiasaura* in that it had a high, crested skull. (*Maiasaura* did not have a crest.) Studying *Hypacrosaurus* will give us even more information about how baby dinosaurs grew up.

ALLOSAURUS

In 1987, in a quarry in Utah, a 150-million-year-old dinosaur egg was discovered. Dinosaur eggs from even earlier times have been found in India. But this one was special. Examining the four-inch-long egg with a CAT-scan, scientists saw it contained a tiny one-inch-long embryo. This is probably the oldest dinosaur embryo ever found. Bones of the flesh eater *Allosaurus* (al-o-SOAR-us) were found nearby. So scientists think it possibly is an *Allosaurus* embryo.

Remember, the biggest dinosaur eggs ever found were the jumbo twelve-by-ten-inch eggs of the forty-foot sauropod *Hypselosaurus*. *Apatosaurus* (uh-pat-o-SOAR-us), a sauropod of the late Jurassic period, was seventy feet long. How big do you think its eggs would be?

Paleontologist Robert Bakker has a surprising answer to this. He thinks maybe *Apatosaurus* babies were *not* hatched from eggs; that maybe *Apatosaurus* mothers gave birth to live babies. What gives him this idea?

Twelve by ten inches is about as big as an egg can be. Any bigger, and the shell would be too thick for a baby to peck its way out. It would also be too thick for oxygen to pass through to the embryo.

The smallest *Apatosaurus* fossil ever found would have weighed about three hundred pounds. It could not have fit into an egg.

And, says Bakker, the female *Apatosaurus* had a large birth canal. So he feels it might have been possible for her to give birth to a large baby.

Big, leaf-eating sauropods such as *Apatosaurus* roamed in herds. Tracks show that the small ones traveled in the center of the herd where they would be safer, the way baby elephants do today.

The *Apatosaurus* baby, Bakker speculates, was probably precocial—able to keep up with the herd soon after it was born. (We know what some present-day precocial babies can do. A baby gnu can get up and walk immediately. A baby whale can keep up with the pod soon after it is born.)

Was this the way it was with *Apatosaurus*? It's remotely possible. But so far, there's no proof. Most other paleontologists say that Bakker has no real evidence to back up this idea. They say the fact that the smallest *Apatosaurus* young found would have weighed three hundred pounds proves nothing. They point out that a newborn *Apatosaurus* baby probably

would have been much smaller. It's just that nobody has found one yet!

It is not totally impossible that *Apatosaurus* mothers gave birth to live babies instead of laying eggs. (A few reptiles do give birth to live young.) But right now even Bakker agrees he needs more positive evidence to back up his theory about *Apatosaurus*.

HOMALOCEPHALE

Homalocephale (ho-mal-oh-seff-AL-ee) was a ten-foot-long "bonehead" dinosaur—so called because it had a very thick skull. It lived 75 million years ago in Mongolia and roamed in large herds. Scientists think *Homalocephale* had head-butting fights with each other, the way sheep and goats do today. And some think it is possible that *Homalocephale* may have given birth to live babies, too.

Why do they think this? The hip bones flared out very wide. This is not true of other dinosaurs. The wide hips would have made it easier for a baby to be born.

Again, there is no proof. It's a possibility.

PINACOSAURUS

In the summer of 1988, in the Gobi Desert of Mongolia, a team of Canadian and Chinese paleontologists found the remains of six *Pinacosaurus* (pin-a-co-SOAR-us) babies.

Pinacosaurus was a type of ankylosaur (ann-KIE-lo-soar), or armored dinosaur. An adult was about eighteen feet long. Its body was covered with tough armored plates. At the end of its tail was a big ball-like club it might have used to swing at attackers.

The baby skeletons were about four feet long (but half of this was made up of tail). Five were huddled together beside an ancient sand dune. The sixth was about twenty feet away. As a team member described it, one was "curled up like a sleeping dog."

The babies were probably less than six months old. They were not yet covered with bony armor, and they had not yet developed a tail club.

Paleontologists used to think that ankylosaurs lived a solitary life. Now, after finding these six young ones together, they are not so sure. Philip Currie, of the Tyrrell Museum of Palaeontology, was part of the expedition. He and the others plan to go back to the site to see if they can learn more about the family life of *Pinacosaurus*.

As new discoveries are made, we keep changing our ideas about dinosaur family life. We are beginning to see that, like animals of today, dinosaurs seem to have had many different ways of protecting their babies and helping them grow up.

Some of the new ideas about dinosaurs are speculation. Others are more certain. But bit by bit, new clues are showing us that dinosaurs—at least some of them—may have done more to care for their young than we ever imagined.

SELECTED BIBLIOGRAPHY

Charig, Alan. *A New Look at the Dinosaurs.* New York: Facts-on-File, 1985.

Coombs, Walter P., Jr. "Juvenile Ceratopsians from Mongolia—the Smallest Known Dinosaur Specimens." *Nature* 283 (1/24/80).

Currie, Philip J. "The Discovery of Dinosaur Eggs at Devil's Coulee." Drumheller, Alberta, Canada: Tyrrell Museum of Palaeontology.

Halstead, L. B., and Jenny Halstead. *Dinosaurs.* New York: Sterling, 1987.

Horner, John R. "Evidence of Colonial Nesting and 'Site Fidelity' Among Ornithischian Dinosaurs." *Nature* 297 (6/24/82).

————. "The Nesting Behavior of Dinosaurs." *Scientific American,* April 1984.

————. "Ecologic and Behavorial Implications Derived from a Dinosaur Nesting Site." In *Dinosaurs Past and Present.* Vol. 2. Seattle, Wash.: Natural History Museum of Los Angeles County/Univ. of Wash. Press, 1987.

Horner, John R., and James Gorman. *Digging Dinosaurs.* New York: Workman, 1988.

Jang, Philip. "Baby Dinosaurs Found in Ancient Sand Dune." *Calgary Herald,* 8/12/88.

Lambert, David (The Diagram Group). *A Field Guide to Dinosaurs.* New York: Avon, 1983.

Ostrom, John H. "A New Look at Dinosaurs." *National Geographic,* August 1978.

Preston, Douglas J. "A Nest of Dinosaurs." *Natural History Magazine,* March 1985.

————. "A Daring Gamble in the Gobi Desert Took the Jackpot." *Smithsonian Magazine,* December 1987.

Wilford, John Noble. *The Riddle of the Dinosaur.* New York: Knopf, 1985.

INDEX